NEW YORK
GIANTS

STEVE POTTS

CREATIVE ✦ EDUCATION

Published by Creative Education
123 South Broad Street, Mankato, Minnesota 56001
Creative Education is an imprint of The Creative Company

Designed by Rita Marshall
Cover illustration by Rob Day

Photos by: Allsport Photography, Associated Press, Bettmann Archive,
Duomo, Focus on Sports, Fotosport, and SportsChrome.

Library of Congress Cataloging-in-Publication Data

Potts, Steve, 1956-
New York Giants / by Steve Potts.
p. cm. — (NFL Today)
Summary: Traces the history of the team from its beginnings through 1996.
ISBN 0-88682-802-3

1. New York Giants (Football team)—History—Juvenile literature.
[1. New York Giants (Football team) 2. Football—History.]
I. Title. II. Series.

GV956.N4P68   1996   96-15225
796.332'64'0974921—dc20

123456

The lady looking out over New York harbor has a face familiar to millions of Americans. The lady's face is on the Statue of Liberty, the beacon that welcomes new American immigrants to the United States. At the base of the statue is a plaque that contains the famous welcome to America's newest residents: "Give me your tired, your poor, your huddled masses yearning to be free."

Just across the bay from the statue is Ellis Island, the small speck of land where millions of immigrants first landed. Those immigrants came from nearly every country in the world. While maintaining their cultural identities, they also embraced many

Defensive back Emlen Tunnell was a Giants record holder.

American customs, including a love for football. And that love for the game was easy to understand for New Yorkers, who loved the team that made the city its home in 1925: the New York Giants.

1 9 2 5

Founder Tim Mara bought the Giants' franchise for a mere $500.00.

THE GIANTS FIND A HOME

When Tim Mara, the team's first owner, bought the Giants for $500 in 1925, America was a very different place. New York was filled with streetcars and Model T cars. Football was mainly a college sport and was played by very different rules. Players played both offensive and defensive, scores were often low, and running, not passing, was the biggest part of the offensive game. Teams were decked out in high-top shoes and leather helmets and wore little padding. They had tough schedules, often playing four games in eight days. Tickets to a football game cost a dollar, a lot of money in 1925, and players earned fifty dollars a game.

The rough and tumble world of football in the 1920s meant that football players had to be tough. Red Badgro, an early Giant, remembered that "Dr. Joe Alexander was coaching the Giants for Tim Mara when I came to them. I had cut my chin open in practice. I needed eleven stitches to close it up. I just went by his office and he didn't have any of his medical equipment with him, so he got a plain needle and sewing thread out of his drawer and sewed up my chin. He liked football more than the practice of medicine, I believe."

Although they had some dedicated, tough players like Badgro, the Giants had trouble keeping a winning coach. Tim Mara went through three coaches in three years and could not find a

Lawrence Taylor was a master of the blitz (page 7).

Quarterback Charlie Conerly passed for over 2,100 yards during the season.

successful leader until he lured Earl Potteiger to the Giants. Potteiger racked up an 11-1-1 record in 1927, but left in 1930. Mara, again without a coach, found Potteiger's replacement in a former Giants player, Steve Owen. Like many early coaches, Owen both coached and played for the team. A careful student of the game, Owen was a dedicated coach. Mara made a wise decision when he gave Owen a long-term coaching contract. Owen would go on to coach the Giants for the next 23 years.

Owen stressed the defensive game. He was responsible for creating the famed "umbrella" defense with a six-man front, one linebacker and four defensive backs. As the quarterback dropped back before passing, two defensive linemen fell back with him and formed a semicircle secondary around him. The three-man formation looked like an umbrella top. The modern 4-3 defense used by teams today grew out of this 1930s formation.

After leading his Giants to six division titles and two league championships and running up a 150-100-17 record, Owen gave up his coaching job in 1953. His 23-year record is still one of the best in pro football history. During his long stint with the Giants, he coached such football greats as quarterback Arnie Herber, defensive back Emlen Tunnell and center Mel Hein. Like his famous players, Steve Owen also made the Pro Football Hall of Fame.

THE GIANTS' GLORY YEARS

A good coach is often known for the skilled assistant coaches he chooses to work under him. Jim Lee Howell, who became the New York head coach in 1954, had the likes of Vince Lombardi, Tom Landry, Dick Nolan and Alex Webster as his assistants. Together with his assistants, Howell turned potential standouts like Frank Gifford into stars.

Gifford came to the Giants out of USC. He was a running back with talent, drive and an "I don't quit" attitude. "Frank was the body and soul of the team," Howell said. "He was the player we went to in the clutch." More often than not, Gifford delivered for his team. In 12 seasons with New York, Gifford led the Giants to five division titles. Along the way he scored 78 touchdowns, including his famous 1956 title game touchdown that gave the Giants the NFL championship over the Chicago Bears.

New York star Frank Gifford made fifty-one pass receptions, gaining over 600 yards.

Gifford also played a part in what became known as the Yankee Stadium Classic, a 1958 game that ranks among the NFL's most famous matchups. On December 28, 1958, the Giants met the Baltimore Colts in the NFL championship game. The player roster looks like a Who's Who of football heroes. Fifteen of that game's players would end up in the Pro Football Hall of Fame. Quarterback Charlie Conerly led the Giants at quarterback. The Colts countered with an offense guided by the great Johnny Unitas and featuring receivers Raymond Berry and Lenny Moore.

Even though it was a rainy day and there was some sloppy play, this game is still regarded by many as one of the greatest in NFL history. Six lost fumbles, a handful of interceptions, and two missed field goals only added to the suspense.

With a 17-14 Giant lead and only three minutes left on the clock, Unitas used three plays to push the Colts 73 yards toward the end zone. When the Colts drive stalled, Lou Michels kicked

Chris Calloway was a dependable receiver (pages 10-11).

1 9 6 0

Kyle Rote was the Giants' top receiver, scoring twenty touchdowns.

a field goal, sending the game into sudden-death overtime. The Colts ran the ball down the length of the field, then set up their last play to look like a Unitas pass. With the Giants defense fooled, Alan Ameche shoved through the Giant line and over the goal line to score a touchdown. The dejected Giants lost to the Colts 23-17.

The Giants were unhappy with their last-minute loss, but their owner Tim Mara was philosophical. "In 1925, we lost to the Bears, but helped save the NFL. Today we lost again, but pro football is the real winner. We may have lost the battle, but we've won the war." The man who helped create modern pro football died only a few weeks later, but Mara leadership continued when his sons took over the Giants.

Jim Lee Howell's stint at New York ended in 1960. When Vince Lombardi refused to leave the Green Bay Packers to take the Giants head coaching job, New York assistant coach Allie Sherman was promoted to head coach. Sherman, a wise observer of the game, saw Charlie Conerly's quarterback skills waning. Sherman went to San Francisco to trade for Y.A. (Yelberton Abraham) Tittle, a player the 49ers felt had outlived his usefulness and was "too old." In 1961, the "old" Tittle led the Giants to a 10-3-1 record and was named the league's Most Valuable Player.

Tittle racked up impressive individual records while leading the Giants to three straight conference titles. Only the NFL championship eluded the powerful Giants. Giants linebacker Sam Huff anchored New York's defense in the early 1960s. His bone-crunching playing style and his inventive way with words pleased fans and sportswriters. Some of his favorite expressions, words like "blitz," "red dog" and "sack," became part of pro football's vocabulary. As coach Sherman said, Huff was "always strong, swift and at the right place at the right time." Despite being a hometown favorite, Huff was traded to the Washington Redskins in 1964. Tittle, his skills fading, retired the following year. This double loss hit the Giants hard. They fell rapidly from the top of the NFL to the bottom, ending the 1964 season at 2-12. Huff and Tittle would be difficult players to replace.

Quarterback Y.A. Tittle passed for 36 touchdowns and over 3,100 yards.

TOUGH TIMES IN NEW YORK

During the next fifteen years, no team had as many good quarterbacks as did the Giants. Five different head coaches went through such standouts as Earl Morrall, Norm Snead, Fran Tarkenton and Craig Morton. But even the best quarterback can't create a winning team without a defense. And a strong defense was what New York so desperately needed.

Desperation leads people to try anything, and the Giants did. They hired coaches. They fired coaches. They drafted, traded and retired players. They even moved the Giants playing field, ending up at the Polo Grounds, at Yankee Stadium, and even at Yale University. Nothing seemed to do the trick. The Giants were going to have to rebuild their team from the bottom up before they became a contender.

The Giants' prospects began looking up when George Young came on board in 1979 as general manager. Young, a careful student of the game, spent the early 1980s trading for and drafting the type of players who would lead the sorry Giants back to contender strength. His first job was to hire a head coach. Young cast his eyes westward and settled on San Diego, where he lured Chargers assistant coach Ray Perkins to New York.

Head coach Ray Perkins joined the Giants to turn the team around.

Young's next acquisition wasn't popular at first with New York fans. Instead of looking to a college football powerhouse for a quarterback, Young and Perkins went to Morehead State College and made Phil Simms their number one pick in the 1981 NFL Draft.

Simms, an unknown when he was drafted, eventually became a key ingredient in the Giants' return to success. But before that occurred, New York needed to do something about its lackluster defense. In 1980 New York's opponents had run up 425 points. The next round of draft picks would have to be used to build up their defense. As it turned out, one of their draft picks would become a legend in New York—and throughout the NFL: Lawrence Taylor.

TAYLOR MAKES THE TACKLES

As a child in Williamsburg, Virginia, Lawrence Taylor intended to become a baseball player. After seeing a few football games, he changed his mind. Eventually L.T., as he came to be called, signed up for a local Jaycees football team so that he could go to Pittsburgh to play. Taylor wanted to see the world and travel, something he had never done before.

His Jaycees coach, Pete Babcock, said "Kid, you're going to be a linebacker." That was fine with Taylor, who began studying for his new job. "I got books out of the school library on linebackers," Taylor remembered. "I read a lot of stuff about Ray Nitschke and Jack Ham and Sam Huff. What I read was how they saw the game, what their feeling was, what their tempo was. I got this concept right then that aside from being smart, a good linebacker was also mean."

After his Jaycees experience, Taylor, now a solid 5-foot-7, 180

David Meggett holds the Giants career touchdown record.   15

1 9 8 0

Hard playing Phil Simms suffered many injuries in his early years.

pounds, found another mentor at Lafayette High School. Lafayette coach Melvin Jones proved an inspiration for Taylor. Taylor described Jones as "a cross between Vince Lombardi and Jesse Jackson. He had all these inspirational sayings plastered all over the walls. One of them really stuck with me: 'If you can perceive it and believe it, then you can achieve it.'"

Five years later, college junior Lawrence Taylor, now 6-foot-3 and 230 pounds, began achieving at the University of North Carolina. By the time he left North Carolina, Taylor was recognized as one of college football's strongest and fastest linebackers hustling. In game after game, his hustling determination produced big plays for North Carolina. During his senior year, an astonishing 33 percent of his tackles were behind the opponent's line of scrimmage. He was an aggressive player who set his sights on winning. Pro scouts flocked to look at the young man they felt would have an easy time adjusting to the rough and tumble world of the NFL.

While Taylor finished college and prepared for the pro ranks, Giants coach Ray Perkins left the pros to coach at the college level in Alabama. Giants management picked Perkins' assistant Bill Parcells as head coach. Shortly thereafter, Parcells and the Giants drafted Taylor. Parcells was not disappointed. During the first week at training camp, a pleased Parcells turned to one of his assistants and said, "I gotta get this kid into the game."

Drafting Lawrence Taylor turned out to be one of New York's wisest decisions. By the end of his rookie year, Taylor had 9.5 sacks, 94 solo tackles and 39 assists. Parcells recalled that Taylor had another talent, too. "What he really did was change the way the other teams looked at our defense. He scared them, is what he did."

Phil Simms was Super Bowl XXI MVP in 1986.

Parcells was in an enviable position. He had a superb offensive leader in Phil Simms and a standout defensive bulwark in Taylor. Simms worked hard to make the Giants offense one of the best in the league. His work ethic impressed his teammates. Receiver Phil McConkey praised the quarterback: "The best thing I can say about Phil Simms is he's the quarterback every lineman would love."

By 1984, Parcells had put together his winning formula. Taylor and Simms maneuvered the Giants into contention for the NFC championship. They won the Wild Card playoff spot and eked out a 16-13 victory over the Los Angeles Rams in the Wild Card game. In the NFC title game, however, Joe Montana escaped Taylor's clutches enough times to lead San Francisco to the title.

The Giants would have to play their best if they wanted to reach the Super Bowl in this competitive atmosphere. In 1985,

though, the Giants weren't playing at their best. They did make it to the playoffs, where they were beaten by Chicago. That was the good news. The bad news was that L.T. was having problems with substance abuse.

Abuse of alcohol and drugs creates problems for many athletes, but L.T. was determined to beat his problem. With faith in his own strength, Taylor began treatment for drug abuse.

When Taylor returned to the Giants, it was with the full support of his teammates and coach. "When he came back," Bill Parcells remembered, "I told him to just play football and I'd do the best to take care of everything else. My job—as a coach and as a friend—was to create the best possible environment for him at that point." With all this support and his own determination, Lawrence Taylor vowed to make 1986 his best year yet. He didn't let his team down.

The Giants seemed unbeatable that year. Phil Simms was at his best throwing and Phil McConkey proved one of the league's best pass receivers. On defense, Taylor again made his presence feared as he menaced opposing quarterbacks. He had 20.5 sacks, nearly toppling the league record, and was named the NFL's Most Valuable Player. He joined only one other defensive player, Alan Page, in winning this high honor.

Taylor's teammates were also making and breaking records. Running back Joe Morris broke his own Giants season record, rushing for 1,516 yards. Giants tight end Mark Bavaro caught 66 passes for 1,001 yards, setting a team record. The 1986 Giants tied the Chicago Bears with a 14-2 mark for the best NFL record.

In the playoffs, the Giants continued their remarkable winning streak. They rolled over San Francisco 49-3 and Washington 17-0 and met the Denver Broncos in Pasadena in the Super Bowl.

1 9 8 6

Bill Parcels was named NFL Coach of the Year.

Mark Bavaro was an outstanding tight end.

That Super Bowl became a showcase for Phil Simms and Phil McConkey. "Conk," as his teammates affectionately nicknamed him, had begun standing on the bench during the regular season and waving his towel to get the fans up out of their seats to cheer on the Giants. Parcells, recognizing what good fan support means to a team, encouraged McConkey to do his towel-waving at the Super Bowl. It worked. Giants fans rocked the stadium with their cheers.

1 9 8 7

Phil McConkey set a team record with nine punt returns in a single game.

The towel wave must have worked on the team, too. Simms completed a remarkable 22 of 25 passes, breaking the Super Bowl record with an 88 percent pass completion mark. His second-half completion of 10 straight passes set another record. Most important for the resurgent Giants, they beat the Broncos 39-20. Simms was named the Super Bowl MVP. There seemed to be nothing that could stop the Giants.

With good luck comes bad, however, and the Giants found that success came and went very quickly. Football commissioner Pete Rozelle had, as one of his goals, the bringing of "parity" to the NFL. He and the team owners got together to use the football draft and their power to draw up tougher schedules for the top teams to make life difficult for the winners. After 1986, it became much more difficult for teams to repeat as Super Bowl champs.

Besides the parity rule, the Giants were also plagued with player problems. Lawrence Taylor had recurring personal problems, Mark Bavaro was involved in a holdout over contract disputes, linebacker Harry Carson retired and injuries hit the Giants hard in 1987 and 1988.

Left to right: Phil Simms, David Meggett, Joe Morris, Lawrence Taylor.

In 1989, the Giants returned to the playoffs primarily through hard work. "We don't have the stars we had on the Super Bowl team," Lawrence Taylor said. "We have a bunch of guys who are just hard workers, guys who want it." Taylor was talking about the young, new players who were bringing another generation of leadership to the Giants.

Parcells began shifting the Giants' philosophy toward ball control. "I knew the game was changing," he said. "There are too many multiple defenses nowadays, too many different fronts. You can't run eight different schemes against eight different fronts. You're better off just lining up with your big guys and pounding away. I knew the game would come to this someday, and I started preparing for it."

With this plan in mind, Parcells began stocking up on powerful offensive linemen. Draft picks like Eric Moore, Jumbo Elliot, Brian Williams and Bob Kratch reflected his decision to beef up his offense. A big front line gave Simms more time to calculate his passing and also opened up holes for runners.

Parcells' strategy worked as the Giants confounded predictions in 1989 and finished their regular season at 12-4 to win their second NFC Eastern Division championship in four years. Thirty-two-year-old veteran running back Ottis Anderson, filling in for an injured Joe Morris, rushed for 1,023 yards. He was aided by rookie David Meggett, who turned in a Giants record with 582 yards in punt returns. The Giants continued their victorious ways in 1990, beginning the season with a 10-game winning streak and finishing with a 13-3 record and another NFC Eastern Division championship.

1 9 8 8

John Elliot was the Giants' second round draft pick.

Quarterback Dave Brown (pages 26-27).

25

Dave Brown is one of the few quarterbacks to earn the starting position so early in his career.

In the playoffs, New York demolished Chicago, 31-3, squeaked by San Francisco, 15-13, and went on to meet Buffalo in Super Bowl XXV. Jeff Hostetler, filling in at quarterback for an injured Phil Simms, threw a 14-yard touchdown pass to Stephen Baker in the second quarter, but Buffalo still held a 12-10 lead at halftime. In the third quarter, the Giants held onto the ball for an amazing fourteen plays before their drive culminated in a one-yard touchdown run by Ottis Anderson. Matt Bahr added two field goals and the Giants eked out a 20-19 victory to give them their second Super Bowl triumph in five years. Anderson was named the Super Bowl MVP.

In the aftermath of this Super Bowl victory came some major changes in the team's management. After 65 years, the Mara family sold their share of the team. The Giants also lost their coach when Bill Parcells resigned. He was replaced by Ray Handley.

For the next two years, injuries plagued the unlucky Giants, causing them to drop from their championship level. Quarterbacks Jeff Hostetler and Phil Simms were amongst the prominent players who lost playing time, while Lawrence Taylor injured his Achilles tendon in a 1992 game against Green Bay. Although he returned to play for one more season, Taylor never regained his earlier form.

The Giants' poor record in 1991 and 1992 led management to fire Handley and replace him with former Denver Broncos coach Dan Reeves. Reeves, who had led the Broncos to three Super Bowl appearances, eagerly accepted the challenge of retooling the Giants and making them into contenders again. In his first year, Reeves guided the Giants to an 11-5 regular season record and a 17-10 Wild Card game victory over Minnesota. Unfortunately, the Giants came up next against the

Rodney Hampton had consecutive 1,000 yard seasons.

Tyrone Wheatley was the Giants' first round draft pick in 1995.

Chris Calloway (#80) celebrates a special teams play with Doug Riesenberg.   31

Cedric Jones brings his defensive skills from the Oklahoma Sooners.

overwhelming force of the San Francisco 49ers and were smashed 44-3. Reeves took the team through a rollercoaster schedule in 1994 that began with three straight wins, ended with six straight wins, but added up to a regular season record of only 9-7. By the end of 1994, both Lawrence Taylor and Phil Simms were no longer in Giants jerseys. An era had ended.

The New York Giants dropped to 5-11 in 1995, but their fans see nothing but a bright future for the young team. Running back Rodney Hampton, a man with a penchant for running and running fast, was a consistent 1,000-yard rusher season after season. Wide receiver Chris Calloway gave the Giants a respected deep-passing threat. The 1995 draft brought New York such bright prospects as running back Tyrone Wheatley, a first round draft pick from Michigan, tackle Scott Gragg, a Montana graduate whose immense size (6-foot-8) and weight (316 pounds) mask surprising speed, and Rob Zatechka, a powerful guard who was plucked from Nebraska's 1995 national collegiate championship team.

Since 1925, New York fans have been loyal to their Giants. The team is steeped in a winning tradition—one that shows every sign of continuing in the 1990s.